Moving Wealth

Tribute

God chose you Sir Markadoo. I have written this book because You are a marker GOD sent me to let me know it is time for me to write this book. The book that lived in me since I was born. Now it is time for me to write the book that I am suppose to write. It may not be the book that others will find FAVOR, but it is the book I was told to write since born. Sir Markadoo, to answer your question, wealth is different to many people. And this book traveled from the depths of my spirit into my soul, so that you can see both of my lives; my life on earth and my life in heaven while I write this book in hope that this marriage of my soul and my spirit can be a new creature. Hopefully, I will give an accurate expression that shares to the world that wealth is many things to one person, and so it is many things to us all. And some of us share their wealth not by food, clothing and shelter, but through ideas and time.

But, we all need to know how to share our wealth with others and still multiply nonetheless. And this expression will be my way of contributing my life into the progress of us all and those who have read my written words. I am not perfect, but I have always been wealthy in an impoverish and violent war zone environment and world of valleys of death. Nonetheless, I enjoy my allies and friendships, bonds with all wealthy beings whether or not they have felt my wealth and favor; it is not my intent to be exposed by everyone. It is my intent to share my presence as I am received. Please continue to join with me in the infinite and immortal journey of MOVING WEALTH.

And Moving Into Wealth

Moving Wealth

In the honor of the Lord of Salvation, our tribes, empires and the ☐ and kingdom of Salvation-Yahweh, we say come into paradise and let us grind, grow and glean together. Honor, Cherish and Serve the "In the Spirit" quickening to understand and to receive the lifestyle and to live the confidence and assurance of life in Paradise. The Move Into the Bodily Temple of Wealth First and then Earthly and Heavenly Wealth.

Introduction

Good morning Students and Mentors:
As one we are one because the Lord gave us the authority to create and restore our world using our gifts. This 40 day fast will be a journey into the depths of self. Finding your creator, the creator of salvation by using the power of your commitment and talents given to you to explore the possibilities of creating new worlds and new strategies.

I welcome you all into the labyrinth of the Merlin and King Arthur Labyrinth. May you come out the other end as whole and holy. Finding your immortality, infinite I Salvation life, wealth and inheritance of endured prosperity, redemption and responsibility. May you engage, commit and endure to the end of the process. Finish the race. Let the 40 day merge you into a new life of brotherhood and sisterhood union with your Creator. Keep your eyes on the prize.

And Moving Into Wealth

Moving Wealth

We invite you to continue to ask, seek and knock for empowerment, stamina and courageous progress and developments. Do not give up. Some days you want to retreat. But hold on. Hold fast. And press forward.

Finish Your Race. And Win. Win daily.

Coach Kay Merchant and Sir Markadoo Haggins
The Merlin and King Arthur Boot camp Complex Model

Table of Content of the 40 Plus Day Labyrinth Fast

The Planning Stage: Brainstorm
January 05th to January 12th 2018
First Week Discussions: In the Spirit Recorded Chat
1st Day Entry: Welcome
2nd Day Entry: Truth and the Mess
3rd Day Entry: The Message and the Tests
4th Day Entry: The Testimony and The Construction
5th Day Entry: Building Blocks
6th Day Entry: Building Wealth Strategies
7th Day Entry: Set Backs and Stay Focus

The Creating and Development Stage
January 12th to January 19th 2018
Second Week Discussions: In the Spirit Recorded Chat
8th Day Entry: The Work and The Grind
9th Day Entry: Learn and Deep Investigation
10th Day Entry: Study and Explore Others Deeply
11th Day Entry: Persistence and Determination

And Moving Into Wealth

Moving Wealth

12th Day Entry: Pity Parties Pitfalls
13th Day Entry: Steadfastness and Will Power
14th Day Entry: Raw Talent and Refinement

The Fashion Design and The Target Practice
15th Day Entry: Aesthetics and Editing
16th Day Entry: Finding Your Expression
17th Day Entry: Creating and Playing
18th Day Entry: Duties and Commitments
19th Day Entry: Engagement and Resilience
20th Day Entry: Challenges and Sabotage
21th Day Entry: Trust and Tread Lightly

The Work Ethics and The Life Studies
22th Day Entry: The Custom Fit
23th Day Entry: Tailor Made
24th Day Entry: Mature and Old Growth
25th Day Entry: Diversification and Purity
26th Day Entry: Traditions and Yesterday Lessons
27th Day Entry: Transformation and Transcending
28th Day Entry: Ascension and Descension

The Journey of Moving Out and The Moving In
29th Day Entry: Saying Goodbye to Old Wealth
30th Day Entry: Good morning: Rise and shine
31th Day Entry: Honeymoon Stage of Wealth
32th Day Entry: The Romance of Wealth
33th Day Entry: The Working Relationship with Wealth
34th Day Entry: Aging with Wealth
35th Day Entry: Renewing of the Vows with Wealth

And Moving Into Wealth

Moving Wealth

Move Into Greatness: Crossing Over
And The Contract to Keep You There
36th Day Entry: Creative and Unconditional Wealth
37th Day Entry: Ironing the Clothes of Wealth
38th Day Entry: Crossing the Red Sea
39th Day Entry: Dress Code and the Code of Wealth
40th Day Entry: Never Leave me or Forsake me Wealth
41th Day Entry: The Knowledge of Yah
42th Day Entry: The Understanding of Yah

Exit Counseling: Congratulations and Celebrate
To the END OF TIME. How to MOVE WEALTH

Notes
Now Begin Your New Life and Chapter into Greatness
and You are Welcome. Always
The M&K/A: Coach K&S Strategy (Merlin & King Arthur:
Kay & Sir Strategy
Coach (Kay) Keisha Lanell Merchant and Coach Sir
Markadoo Haggins

January 10th we met
12th we started talking on the phone
15th recording was born
15th the book was birth after two days of conversation.
Fast began 15th and now 19th it has been 5 days into the
actual fast and recordings or commitment of coaching into
the Merlin and King Arthur Coaching Sessions.

And Moving Into Wealth

Moving Wealth

Just our minutes for this far. Vision building a joint venture for Moving Into Greatness
And Building a Service Learning University for Apprenticeship Programs
World Tours for Speaking Engagements with Students and Mentors
Teaching How to Move Into Wealth and Greatness
Build a Curriculum and Wellness, In the Spirit and Fitness Programs
Create a website, help desk and hot-line for our members.

This textbook is to assist you as a tool to become awakened to LOVE. Love Prevails All. And it is LIVING. Love is not abusive, controlling or exploiting even it is not violating. It is the conversation, keep your hands and feet to oneself, and using the power of your thoughts and words to MOVE WEALTH and to MOVE INTO WEALTH to use Your Favor to heal yourself, your tribes and the worlds you live in TODAY and every day. Never leaving you or Forsaking your mission to MOVE WEALTH, the LIVING.
Motif: Paradise Living

In the Spirit of Harriet Tubman
Every great dream begins with a dreamer. Always remember, you have within you the strength, the patience, and the passion to reach for the stars to change the world. ~Harriet Tubman
Read more at:
https://www.brainyquote.com/authors/harriet_tubman

And Moving Into Wealth

IN THE SPIRIT CHATS JR.: MODULE 1

Journal Entry 1 Welcome Orientation

I am so excited to share with you my 40 days with Sir Markadoo. What an honor and blessing to have the Lord bring this God's Professional through my path in these 40 days. I wanted to create a book that would be my Noah's Ark and my Abraham's Altar. I could not help myself the day I received a vision of inspiration to write this book, so I wanted to take the time to say Welcome into my life for 40 days featuring Sir Markadoo, the author of Economics Evangelism. I am so excited to Move Greatness. Let us begin the journey. I wanted to share the spiritual side of capitalism, money and all the dirty laundry inside of greatness. The cleaning house process that we all have encountered when cleaning mess, and we all know what it means when you own a big house. The bigger the house; the more responsibility and work to clean the house. I remember when I was a child, cleaning homes, I thought to myself "Why in the world, would anyone want a huge home?" As a child, it was so much work for my little hands. But imagine the organization system that adults use to

Moving Wealth

build and clean homes; it makes it easy and reasonable to expand your territories. I wanted to take my time to talk about Noah and Abraham in their journey of cleaning their home.

I know that many people these days do not read the bible. It is actually something of the essence, and not the fun read as when I was a child; exploring and discovering the world that saved us from death. It felt as though people persecuted the innocent based on the reasons of lack of responsibility of their wealth. The people of God did not know how to move their wealth. They were not able to learn quickly enough to move wealth. Earth bending, water bending and fire bending in the fun and innocent cartoons, show people that moving their talent is very useful and constructive when helping the world stay centered and responsible. It was with this thought that I delved into what happens when you are without money and power even privileges that societal norms gives as an asset to food, shelter and clothing; the opportunity of freedom and pleasure. I am sure that in this journal entry that my conversation about what I am so excited about in these 40 days that we are moved in one element as to God is our wealth. We always have to wonder what manifest in earth; did it manifest in the heavens. The celestial world

And Moving Into Wealth

Moving Wealth

of God and creation begins with the questions that we are wealthy for what reasons and what are we suppose to do with wealth?

I know that people want to discuss about how we use wealth, and how we have the right and freedom to waste our wealth on pleasure and the construction of identity is not based on tradition but based on the complications of peer pressures. Do we understand the need to be approved and accepted by our peers? We never talk about peer pressure, and we never really understood why this matters. I have investigated the two stories for the parable and morale of the story. The message I wanted to glean as this is the first day of my 40 days that Noah was not interested in the life of his family. He was interested in the death of his family. Why do I talk about life as we can honestly state that life is a form of wealth. We know that Noah was pushed into a covenant with God not from choice but obligation, need and even desperation. Noah was concerned not by his assets in life, but the wealth of can I save my family from their death or premature death? It was like sitting in front of the screen wondering as a spectator will God save these men and women who were innocently killed by terrorism or military and policing. I wonder would these accidents happen to more populations

And Moving Into Wealth

Moving Wealth

as the world become infected by haunting of internal soul torments to kill, be violent and stir up trouble.

Journal Entry 2: Truth and the Mess

Now I've been free, I know what a dreadful condition slavery is. I have seen hundreds of escaped slaves, but I never saw one who was willing to go back and be a slave.
Read more at:
https://www.brainyquote.com/authors/harriet_tubman

It is that time of the year that I wanted to create and invent. I know people ask me all the time is, "Why did I go to school? I felt that education as to knowledge and understanding was owning eternal wealth. Understanding what I can after getting trained into a discipline. I saw it as learning how to build a craft, and achieving greatness through mastering a craft. I saw myself go into the forestry recreation and management, but I saw that the Lord Almighty had other plans for my life. I assure you that learning how to build Eco-systems was my ideal work in the fields. Unfortunately, they did not see my vision. I was not offered a scholarship, grant or work study. I was left in the cold trying to figure out how I would influence all populations even the elite that my

And Moving Into Wealth

Moving Wealth

education can be useful. I had to prove that my craft was useful to God and to creation. I had to find favor by asking them to help. I had to remind them their loyalty. I bet they laughed at me. I was asking for loyalty from people who were giving them loyalty. It was me that did not have the understanding of what is commitment and engagement. I could barely understand difficulty. I remember that success may not always mean popularity, fame and riches. It is the availability to study, investigate and invest in the opportunities of self, your tribes and the worlds to come.

Journal Entry 3: The Message and the Tests

I was the conductor of the Underground Railroad for eight years, and I can say what most conductors can't say; I never ran my train off the track and I never lost a passenger.
Read more at:
https://www.brainyquote.com/authors/harriet_tubman

      Sometimes in life the messages from the Mighty God of Salvation pushes us in ways we cannot understand. I am sure that we all have some radical experiences that left us crying at night. Confused. Hurt. Scared. I want to remind us all that we cannot move forward without sitting in the room in our life that we can move forward with power

And Moving Into Wealth

Moving Wealth

only if we can build our relationship with God, our God of Salvation. We can sit in the throne room of the Salvation until we can receive our wealth. The wealth to breathe. The wealth to live holistically in our lives without the worries of devastation. Our devastation comes from the lack of experiences we have with our creator of salvation. The creator of salvation is the only key to our wealth. What kind of wealth are we trying to access? The wealth of salvation is a paradise that we can only afford with the approval, acceptance and compassion of the God that created it so. When we talk about money, economics, we have talk to talk about scarcity. We have to talk about the many errors we face in our dysfunctional lives. We survive and we excel. Today we have to be able to transcend in our systems that we face the most errors in our life. The error of discrimination. The error of hate crimes. The error of defection. It is with this purpose we have to understand that the wealth of salvation comes with a world of the unknown in the mind. The power to be part of a tree of life. The tree of life that gives eternal life with thoughts. The picture of life that salvation comes from the creator of Salvation. The salvation is paradise. Paradise as Isaiah shared in Isaiah 55 and 58 we have to foreshadow that wealth comes from God the creator of salvation, restoration, regeneration and Eternal

And Moving Into Wealth

Moving Wealth

Life. We have a soul in this world to understand that we have weaknesses. Those weakness leads us to come to an acknowledgment of two things. We need wealth of God or wealth of money.

      Let us understand the wealth of God in salvation is not having money. The reason people are anger because they want to understand that pain, suffering and death could be part of our salvation which is why we have to delve into the truth of errors which we call sins. We live in a world of errors. We can provide ourselves with God's wealth which is his inspired thoughts that lead us to everlasting fountains of water to quench our thirst, everlasting motivation to satisfy our stomachs and everlasting assurance to provide us the will power and courage to live above our social rejection and persecution. The wealth of money is our ability to provide for our families and for our own lives through the sacrifice of having quality time speaking to our God of salvation. We are challenged by our literature to create new worlds. WE are challenged by our thinkers to create new life. We are challenged by our money to provide and when money fails us; we blame humanity, the system and all the institutions for not giving us enough resources to provide us what we are seeking in our souls the needs and desires to be satisfied.

And Moving Into Wealth

Moving Wealth

We blame God the salvation to create new opportunities with our money, with our system and with our future, but in honesty we should ask our God of salvation to change the game and for us to be game changers. The master piece for paradise, trees that give us an ageless life. The herbals to cleanse us from diseases. The celestial angels to guard our steps. The courage to trust us to be citizens of a system without errors. We have to understand that the order of salvation means we have to be filled with the ideas of paradise. We have to be filled with the ideas of salvation. We have to be filled with the thoughts of wealth of the new Jerusalem that creates in us a testimony and the construction to live in new territories. The day our messages from God and our tests from God which are our lemons will turn into lemonade.

Journal Entry 4: The Testimony and The Construction

Knowledge is powerful. We feed from the trees of knowledge of good and evil. We delve into the ideas of what is good for us and what is evil and destructive for our own lives. We have to purchase the provisions in this life and to be citizens of capitalism; we have to move into the wealth of

And Moving Into Wealth

Moving Wealth

capitalism. We have to buy into the costs of capitalism. We have citizens who need capitalism to survive. They feed and drink capitalism daily. I spent 20 years of my life learning the ideas of business. The world of business in capitalism suggests that we are workers that provide two engines into life. The first engine was capitalism and the second was celestial.

The wealth from the celestial kingdom does not come in our lives without petition, prayer, steadfastness, honesty and some strong passion for what we truly want. It will be one thing for sure that no one will leave this life saying they did not passionately live their heart consciousness. They will see who they truly are and who they are in the world and in their inner strength of the neediness and grittiness of the soul for labor pains to what an individual want whether it is hungry for food, hungry for shelter or hungry for love. It is the neediness for the thing you cannot have, and leave this world petitioning to the celestial kingdom to intervene and showmanship of how it is expressed and received. The wealth digging experience in your soul to see whether or not your soul has the treasure that you believe is inside. The wealth that is given to us before we were born. The wealth is in our soul. Why is our soul the mansion? Why is our

And Moving Into Wealth

Moving Wealth

soul the storehouse of the treasures? Understanding the power of the soul that the God of salvation has given. We fight and wrestle all the days of our life just to die in our poverty. The day we face the truth about our reality in this earth. We can support the ideas that externally we have capitalism, but do we understand the internal wealth of capitalism of the God of Salvation?

The power that the God of Salvation put deep in our souls. What can I say but what can we do if we spend a lifetime without pulling out the diamonds in our soul while we pushing diamonds outside of our soul.

Journal 5th day entry: Building Blocks

Sometimes in life you want to build, but you have forces that won't let you build. Your territories may be as small as an ant, but even the ants build colonies. I am sure in this life; I have learned you must micro and macro all you can in your words and thoughts. Your words are the world as the stars are to the galaxy. The day that I realize that the words and thoughts became the power, wealth and food that I could not have or eat. I was changed in a twinkling in the eye. I started to cash

And Moving Into Wealth

Moving Wealth

in all my pain, fears and devastation for the opportunity to be strategic my life for the world of words and thoughts. Let me explain, it was the glory of God to listen and understand all the wonderful leaders who set the world right. They had words and their thoughts that were rich and well established in their souls. They started to break the silence by sharing to the world their dreams and hopes even wants. This materialized into the world we live in as their work changed the face of American people as well as those around the world. I am not going into the minds and hearts of these leaders. Their are plenty books that focus on these giants of thinkers and speakers, and that is not the point of this journey. The point of this journey is the process, and how to saturate yourself in the construction of these words, but also how to build from the building blocks of words. The micro management of words means to delve into the way you use words. The way you use your thoughts. The ideology around seek ye first the kingdom of God and his righteousness and then all things will come. What did this mean? It had appeared of thousand of times that the Word of the lord did not come back in void. By his word, he created. I have seen this happen so many times. I have seen the word that comes out of the mouth and heart, feed lives, and yet the soul that had thought it and

And Moving Into Wealth

Moving Wealth

spoken that word still did not or could not feed their own life and their own household. You have to ask yourself, what is the risk and burden of being a healer? The life of not having the opportunity that you give to others. This journey is to give you the opportunity to MOVE WEALTH and to MOVE INTO WEALTH.

Pack up your bags healer, and move into wealth. How do we change the game for our own lives. It is a duty for us to MOVE WEALTH for others, and to help others to MOVE INTO WEALTH. It is not taught to healers how to MOVE WEALTH and MOVE INTO WEALTH for their own lives and their tribes. Now my intent is to show the world how to do that. LOVE THYSELF as you would LOVE OTHERS. Let us talk about loving thyself. The building blocks of life is to understand the steps of loving thyself. How can you love thyself if you do not know what love is? How can you love others if you do not and have not had love? Let me ask you, what is wealth? Is it minerals, rocks and dead trees, and solicit others to give you power, money and territories, or opportunities? Let us start with how do you MOVE WEALTH healer for your own life and for the life of your households.

And Moving Into Wealth

Moving Wealth

What is the building blocks that I am talking about in this journey? I am talking about the crawling stage in life. How do we work on the motor skills of the healer? This journey is the conversation you have with yourself and God. It is the out of body experience you have in your life with the conversations you have with your creator. The way we talk to ourselves and the way we talk to God in our minds and in the mirror. We must learn to record our conversations at least once in your lifetime. Healing is not giving people opportunities to do their own desires, but healing others is to give people the chance and change to help others, their own lives, their tribes, and then reach out and serve their neighbors, and the dying world until the work is finished.

Here is the building blocks, the intent. "I do not answer you when you talk to me because the knowledge I give to you will not be used correctly." This is the creator's way of teaching us how to build using the blocks given to us. We have to learn how to watch and examine the intent we choose to do things. I had to confess sometimes in these confessions that my intent started with the first thoughts and these first thoughts grow like weeds, and then when they do not manifest, we wonder what happened? These weeds killed our crops as

And Moving Into Wealth

Moving Wealth

they become invasive and invasion. These thoughts were ignored. We did not up root these thoughts and conversations by correction. What is correction? The process of examining the why we shared those things and spoke even those things. It was an example when I was a child, I was told that I would never be an executive or commander in chief. Then I started to say, I would not want to own WEALTH. I could not understand why I had that thought? Here is another statement given to me as a child. I was not going to live a full life or a forever life. We all die. Then I started to not want to own the opportunity to MOVE WEALTH or to MOVE INTO WEALTH. It did not dawn on me that my environment planted seeds. But, here is the power move in my life. The creator of my soul, whispered a WORD in me that no one knew was spoken. YOU ARE MY SPECIAL ELECT, and I CHOSE YOU. "My grace is enough." Then, I saw a warrior rise up in me, and I started to create as co-creator a new WEALTH. For the traditional wealth had gatekeepers that planted seeds that I would not be CHOSEN, and I had to be violent and take it by FORCE.

Let me remind you this is not for everyone. This is for the healers who had words spoken to them in their environments that were hostile war

And Moving Into Wealth

Moving Wealth

zones. These are the ones who had two whispers in the ears. The cartoons of a hostile take over and the gentle angelic celestial being correct by kissing your wounds and said, you will be well. Have you ever been loved by the LIVING GOD? This is the building block that will change your life. Your years of crawling in this hostile world in war zones, but your life on the inside someone speaking to you the joy, love and sing to you when you sleep. Someone who takes you to a place that is beautiful, rich and full of love, life and enchantment, that all the books in this life could not explain the reality inside your soul. I believe they call this entity the COMFORTER, but I am calling her WEALTH. Someone that never leaves you or forsake you.

Sometimes people talk about having a voice guide them, and help them achieve all their goals, hopes and wishes. But, have you ever had someone that whispers enchanting love and romance you day to day, saying sweet loving things that you are beautiful while your oppressors spit hate until you bleed in your mind? It is like you have a place to escape to and all your drawings, creative scripts and imaginations of fictional tales cannot do it justice, but the way WEALTH whispers to you while you play with your building blocks. Healers, you heal others, but often times you do not heal yourself or

And Moving Into Wealth

Moving Wealth

your tribe because you fail to realize that what you have practiced on others you need to practice on yourself. You cannot always spend your time in your enchanted world with WEALTH, but you need to MOVE you and your family INTO WEALTH. Moving wealth is the day you begin to romance and speak sweet things to WEALTH. You must learn how to MOVE WEALTH not with flattery, but with the love that was given to you. You must give it back to WEALTH, her. I often call WEALTH my heavenly father and mother, heavenly parents. It is obvious that we spend our whole lives not equally bound to the parental care in earth or in heaven. But, to use our conscious to equally bound them all together as one team, can create the opportunities to MOVE WEALTH and to MOVE INTO WEALTH for the healer and my tribes, your tribes while under hostile take over and in war zones, under the oppression that the world is bearing rotten fruit.

Journal Entry 6th day entry: Building Wealth Strategies

In this world, we have to ask ourselves how are we building wealth? What are the things we strategist when we think about wealth? I have examined the world and watch people spend their wealth. They have paid for homes, clothing, shelter

And Moving Into Wealth

Moving Wealth

and property. Some have created inventions that killed people and destroyed the planet even the atmosphere. I have seen most populations including myself spend their wealth to feed themselves with the basic needs in life, to feel secure and safe. I have seen the world receive the opportunities and luxury to feel approved and to feel achieved by their goal setting being accomplished. I have seen these strategies even go as far as killing sprees and violent rapes, and wastes to harm others. I have been asked what would I do with my wealth? I have took my whole life in this journey to finally expose that truth and that mystery. I remember as a child, the seeds planted was the communication system of the TOWER of BABEL. It was the first COMMUNICATION SYSTEM in our written journal which most populations have now written it off as a children's book or children's story book. But, it still allows me to explore the possibilities of what will I do with my wealth? We all get to answer this question. I remember as a child, I too wanted the same opportunities on the Maslow's pyramid to achieve the actualization that this world sought after. I wanted to follow the paths of my ancestors, and that desire changed the game for me. I started to hunger for a different type of food, a different type of clothing and a different type of housing. And such

And Moving Into Wealth

Moving Wealth

a different type of goals, yet I recognized as a healer that I still was split in two from my earthly soul and my heavenly soul. How could I be two people in one world?

    I have two souls into one body. The soul of the earth and the soul of the heavens? Most people may call this a psychological problem, but yet, I realize a very unique powerful epiphany that psychologically, people were here in two lives and this was a brain injury. But this brain injury was designed by the humanity words and from the humanity's lack of resources to understand the power of two heads are better than one when trained, coached, and educated with the right leaders, teachers and trainers. We are worried about what we have lacked, but we do not change our attention to what we have gained. I want to be healthy in all cases. So, what happens when mental illness becomes a new world of existence based on the alteration of the brain due to chemicals, eating toxins, and so our souls adapt to the new existence and to the changed environment forced. What happens when PURITY has vanished and DIVERSITY has arrived? No longer, no one is PURE. No longer NO ONE is PERFECT. Now we live in a world that we have brain injuries, and people are living with a brain with eyes and others

And Moving Into Wealth

Moving Wealth

are living with brains without eyes. The MUTATION and adaption changes things. Diversity is BORN. The first strategy of wealth building is how do we MOVE WEALTH?

Journal 7th day entry: Set Backs and Stay Focus

Daily, I share people getting people to approve of you in the environment that you live in as though FAVOR is what gives us wealth. I remember having approval of men, but then you have the violations that came with being approved by defective and dysfunctional environments that exploit your innocence. It is not the ability to attain wealth, but the ability to be approved by the one who owns wealth. We sell and trade, and those who multiply wealth through selling their skills, talents and interactions whether through human capital or capital, they would convince everyone that using the bootstraps kept them wealthy. They forget it is not by the wealth that makes one wealthy but by the FAVOR shown to them, and then they choose to be wasteful, a horde or a healer. But even healers corrupts when placed under FAVOR. The power of understanding the word and the world of words means to understand the power of WEALTH.

And Moving Into Wealth

Moving Wealth

Not just FAVOR but the opportunity of WEALTH living in your blood. The power of wealth means to be present in the future, past and present in one space while selling and trading even interacting. It is not to possess objects. It is not the possession of objects or ownership of objects, but to MOVE WEALTH and to MOVE INTO WEALTH. The set backs of owning possessions have been known by most people who have died. They have stated in many episodes that they leave wealth behind. WEALTH can not go where they are going. They mentioned WEALTH as though it stays in earth. This is the WOLF in SHEEP clothing. Leaving behind wealth as though the wealth they owned was not theirs, and it would not leave earth. This wealth left them and forsaken them when they had to journey to the grave. This "WEALTH" allowed them to have the parental provisions in earth but not in the grave or heaven and thereafter. Stay focus now. We just begun. The wealth we must learn is not in earth or in heaven. The wealth many left behind was dead and not alive. Stay focus. Do not get distracted.

Stay focus is the opposite side of Set Back. We must learn how to Stay Focus. Fasting is a technique and tool to learn how to elevate yourself

And Moving Into Wealth

Moving Wealth

when your environment is in chaos, but you are FOCUS.

This is the right passage to WEALTH. Some people stay in a position that getting to wealth is enough, but moving wealth is not in their best interest or moving into wealth is a goal set by their intent. I am sure healers receive wealth, and they spend their wealth healing others, but yet they do not heal themselves or their own tribes. Why is that? They have the set back of leaving themselves behind and their own tribes. This is the process of fasting and prayers. We call this meditation. We call this chanting. We call this mantras. We call this MOVING WEALTH. We are learning how to move the chi which is the living and fire breathing energy of light. Some may call it the complete atom. But in the righteous standpoint, the right to move wealth is not getting up in the morning and using capitalism to spend money, sell goods and products only, as though we not only eat bread daily, but we also live through the word of the living Yah. This is different then the living God, which we understand God as the being of the universe, and those that understand God understand God as the creator and design even owner of all things, of the living. And then there is the SON of GOD the owner of the dead. Together as one, they

And Moving Into Wealth

Moving Wealth

can express the things of GOD and the SON of God, but we miss out on the opportunity to understand YAH. Who is Yah? Yah is the Spirit that moves GOD and the SON of God even all things. What movement happened when the dead is quickened. What does it mean to be quickened by the Yah?

It is the YES. It is the YES in all that you do not based on the righteousness, but based on the Comforter to be the Merlin icon or the Teacher in You, the Trainer in You and the Authority in You that guides you and guards you, so you can change, transform and transcend into the Final You. The Purposeful You and the Day You Move Into Wealth. And forever live as one. Wealth becomes one with you through marriage and through estate. Then you can eat, drink and be merry for you have all your needs supplied by the springs of the Word and Thought in You; created by You. This is the day that your blood and water becomes regenerative and power that provides for you and enchantment is born through you. Never again will you trade and sell dead objects and your net worth and your worth will not be based on dead materials, but based on the living materials in You. What living materials am I talking about? I am talking about the conversation you have with Yah, and the celestial

And Moving Into Wealth

Moving Wealth

creator who birth you and those conversations that you have daily with those that knew you since the beginning of time and to the end of time. These conversations are gold nuggets. These conversations are rubies. These conversations are worth more than any wealth in earth and all the wealth prior or thereafter. These conversations are counted and valued at infinite value. This is the wealth that paid the price for your sins by the first conversation of the Son and the Father with Yah. For they Moved Wealth into the Son, and the Son was quickened by Wealth at death; chosen to be the God of the Dead. The God of the Living and the God of the Dead moved wealth to serve you: this is the everlasting covenant, and one day, you will move wealth to let you move into wealth and become one forever.

      And this is called Happily Ever After. The End. This is the day there is no more crying. This is day there is no more pain. This is day there is no more suffering. This is the day no more starvation. This is the day that there is no more death. This is the day that your corruptible life is swallowed up by the incorruptible existence of becoming one with Yah. This is the day that the Co-Creator God and Feminine Aspect of the Godhead becomes One with You and you become the Daughter of God. The

And Moving Into Wealth

Moving Wealth

daughter of God, bride of God, and so your duties with wealth will be to quicken others. Men and women who are moving wealth and move into wealth will be called the God of the Quickening and your sister is called the God of the Roaming. Yes, a new children's story for all will come as they are and learning to be teachable and students may start with learning the truth of what is animate and what is inanimate. But, you on the other hand do not make animate objects or inanimate objects. But...You just move them both into Wealth using your conversations to Yah. And Yah quickens them.

Moving wealth is to stay focus and not allow your setbacks to distract you from moving the chi and using the chi to do greater feats.

THE CREATING AND DEVELOPMENT STAGES: MODULE 2

8th Day of Journal Entry: The Work and The Grind

And Moving Into Wealth

Moving Wealth

The work is not that you have to pay taxes and to follow a leader. The work is to have the conversations that no one has inside you and find Yah, and when you find Yah, to speak to Yah's heart and speak to Yah's mind, so Yah can Move. Moving Wealth is a living breathing Being that is more powerful than a dragon. It is all creations Eternal Mother, Infinite Mother, Immortal Mother, it is the creator WOMB that birthed all creation through her Cells. Moving Into Wealth is that day you moved into her cells, and in nine months as your earthly mother moved you through her WOMB, so did Yah, she moved you through her WOMB. Now Moving Wealth is not a practice of exploitation, theft or manipulation or even FORCE. It is a loving relationship of romance, intimacy and strong bonding time that you and Yah conversion through conversation that You are after her own heart as Favored and teachable as you can be to become one. You must understand that in this life if you do not have a conversation with Yah; you have not had the privilege or honor to have Wealth. One conversation with Yah, Abba and the Son of God, meant you explored the possibilities in your imagination that you are more than human.

That is the work and the grind to understand that you are more than human not like super powers, super authority or super superficial, but

And Moving Into Wealth

Moving Wealth

super intimate with the creator that moves you into life. It is not that you have pain, suffering and starvation as to the lack of resources and safety, but that your mind, heart and soul even spirit can wrap its life around the concept that you may be more than human. That you may have four parents not just one set of parents but two set of parents. The first set gives you a shell to live, and the other gives you wealth to move and to be one forever. Many of us miss out the opportunity to move wealth or to move into wealth, but honestly, Wealth chooses you. You must return the FAVOR and choose WEALTH. The first day that you choose wealth it is a work day. The day you choose wealth it is hard working and at the end of the work day then it becomes a grind. The grind is not the same as the work. The work is to CHOOSE wealth, and the grind is to MOVE wealth. The movement of wealth has been an ancient practice since the beginning of time by many cultures which they may call it the moving of the chi. This is not the final realization because moving chi is like moving water or moving furniture. No one understands the misconception of moving chi or moving wealth. It is not an aimlessly moving wealth like roaming minutes on a cell phone. It is not wealthy people moving absent mindedness inanimate objects or exploiting human capital through force and

And Moving Into Wealth

Moving Wealth

violence as we have seen over the years in history, but moving wealth as we have seen may created traditions of strengths and weaknesses or predators and prey, as though victimization and perpetrator allowed people to die at the hands of vulnerability and ignorance. "For my people are ignorant, and so die." It is not decaying, aging and dying as we see death from the lack of resources and lack of knowledge as our traditions blinds us to believe and understand. Moving inanimate objects as we have done with cars, homes and budgets as if we can keep "wealth" through selling and buying of goods and humans. This is the errors of humanity. But when you are more than human, you understand the truth of the behind scenes of moving wealth.

You move wealth not by FORCE, but through LOVE. People say LOVE PREVAILS. Then they spend their whole lives loving creation and humanity, but they forget to love Yah and the God of the Living and the God of the Dead. They forget that moving wealth through their three WISHES is all they have known and have been taught that they miss out on the opportunity to work for Yah and grind for Yah. They lose out on the opportunity to be employed by God of the Living and the God of the Dead. They forget to be an

And Moving Into Wealth

Moving Wealth

employer with the GOD of the living and the God of the Dead, and Yah the God of Wealth who is LOVE. Love prevails. Wealth prevails. She prevails not because she was forced, deceived or tricked. She prevails because she understands who you are for she carried you 9 months in her WOMB. And birthed you, and you are hers. She is prevailing in you not because you Love others, but you loved her first. You Chose her first. You spent your life moving wealth by giving her your time, your energy and your love. You spent all those hours that you could be selling and buying goods and gave up your life to sit at her feet and learned of her. You meant to tell her a story, but you chose to listen to her story. You moved her not because you did anything right. You moved her because you understood one thing only, and that without her. Life is not exciting, motivating and alive without her. She is the essence and the Sweet Sauce in LIFE. Moving wealth is not getting her to do what you tell her to do as though you have the authority and power to have FAVOR by cunning words or sweet words. It is the understanding and knowledge that putting her first and being teachable means everything can be given to you properly in the right time. And you become one with WEALTH through her and in her and wealth is nothing without her. It is useless and empty

And Moving Into Wealth

Moving Wealth

without her. Life is empty, living is empty and all that you are or become without her is without arousal, romance and

the honeymoon in you. Moving wealth means to understand working for her and grinding for her is not moving into wealth or moving wealth. Spending time with Yah. Using up your time to spend with her means giving up your life to meet someone special and worthwhile. Meeting someone who is beautiful in every way. And after spending time, having conversations, and then falling out of love from being in love, then you will know her. At that moment, only at that moment, then can you know if you was chosen to LOVE her forever. If you move wealth at that moment after all said is done, and after receiving all the secrets, all the passion and all of her, at that moment, falling out of love with her, being familiar with her, and knowing everything about her, and then you are not excited. And then you are not interested in her, and then you want to move on without her. You will Move Out of Wealth or Move Into Wealth. Moving wealth to share everything on her mind, everything in her heart, and you get to have the privilege and honor to know and understand wealth which leads you to fall in love with Yah, and wealth is who she is a storehouse of all things, then you allow yourself to fall out of love with her because she becomes

And Moving Into Wealth

Moving Wealth

common, familiar and no longer excited. Your heart wax old, and dies for her love, then you will Move Into wealth or you will Move out of wealth. This is the day that happens once in every lifetime. This is the appointed day that change happens forever. This is the day, some call it a death or an everlasting life. Some are redeemed and some are not. This is the day that life changes forever. This is the appointed day that moving wealth is not enough. Having wealth is not enough. And spending wealth is not enough. Saving wealth is not enough. And forcing others to attain wealth is not enough. Everything done in the name of GETTING wealth is not enough. As King Solomon stated in his romantic novella, that awakened love is not enough. It is like a fire that burns down everything. Not because of jealous, or anger or death, but by CHOICE. This is the day that moving wealth is not enough. Moving into wealth becomes one choice in a lifetime and many know wealth and understand wealth, and get familiar with wealth, and now they do not value wealth or find her worthy of their time and energy. Yah is Love. And true wealth is not lovely unless your eyes see beauty forever.

This is when it is written the dog returns to its vomit; and leaves wealth, love and Yah. And

And Moving Into Wealth

Moving Wealth

moves out forever. The moment that you have experience the King Arthur moment that you have been graciously given all power, all knowledge and all understanding even all glory by being coached, trained and taught by Yah in earth which is your soul's life and in heaven which is your spirit's life, as one a married life as the new creature we call the elected. Yah raised you, saved you and provided for you. And now, you turned into the Merlin, the sorcerer, and used the wealth to exploit, force, violently shed blood, and spend on lavish and heavenly things, and finally, receiving all the pleasures, spoiled riches from what blood buys, and all the ectasy of earth and in the heavens, you are left with this last truth that you had a life as a Merlin in the spirit and a life of King Arthur in the body. And after it is all said and done, you divorce her, and walk away from Yah. Walk away from Love. Those may say what if you did not do that. The question is not what you did with your season with Wealth, moving wealth. The question is what did you do after it was all said and done? Did you leave? Did you forsake Yah? Did you spend your time with her? Did you spend endless hours with her daily? Did you have conversations as you have done from the beginning, in the journey and in the passion? Did you lean on Yah always? The blasphemy of Yah is not that you left her. The

And Moving Into Wealth

Moving Wealth

blasphemy of Yah is that you can never come back because your heart lost interest in her and forever have the eyes of discontent for her. By knowing all of her, and understanding all of her, you do not see anything special about her, or exciting about her, and so you see her as useless and you have no use of Yah. Yah is no longer useful to you, and that is how you know that you worshiped what she was able to give. You valued what she could do for you and not what you could do for her. You missed the opportunity to understand what it means to share your life with her as she spent her whole life sharing her life with you. As you say goodbye to her; the work and grind of creating and developing YOU is complete. You leave without saying thank you and good bye. In your eyes, you are done with boot camp.

9th Day Journal Entry: Learn and Deep Investigation

Sometimes it takes deep revelations from saturating and sitting with information you have discovered in your life. Exploring all the

And Moving Into Wealth

Moving Wealth

possibilities of the information given to you. Whether it is a lie or truth, fact or fiction and evidence and belief. It is a world of wonderful imaginative worlds that can be explored and outcomes from sitting with these diversified data and knowledge base. It is obvious that all time and history is developed by a standpoint and a view of someone who spoke it to the universe. It transpires from thought into the spoken word and in the spoken word it develops into an implementation process. The road of greatness may not be achieved, but it is realized as we take the journey that the word creates.

10th Day Entry: Study and Explore Others Deeply

We have to learn how to explore others deeply. We have to learn how to have techniques to investigate with our eyes, our minds, our nose, our ears and our hearts. We have to realize in this life time, we are entertaining angels. We have to be aware that we are intently digging for the depth of the message whether it is nonverbal and verbal. We must understand the importance of collecting information and what happens after we collect

Moving Wealth

information we must know what to do with that information.

11th Day Journal Entry: Persistence and Determination

One of my favorite stories that I read over and over was David and the Goliath. Of course now knowing more about history, I am sure it was a black on black combat. Nonetheless, what I adored about both of these men were that they gave their lives for their faith. They were confidence about what they were doing. They showed no doubt. They were fearless for the evidence and information they have collected to perform and do what they considered as their life work and life destiny. I have experienced many years the opportunities to be humbled and proud. It has taught me that confidence is persistence and determination. It is separate from Humility and Pride or Proud. It is the ability to stay focus on something as if you was driven to the end of time with it. It is something powerful to be driven about something that is worthy and valuable to be given the attention of our souls. Wealth and something about capitalism that drives people to kill, steal and destroy. Greed is the

And Moving Into Wealth

Moving Wealth

biggest issue of wealth in capitalism. The greed becomes wasteful and mismanagement of funds through greed seems to be the problem. The environment can be construed based on lack of ethics that consist of personal options and personal discretion. We have talked about this issue since the beginning of conception on the decision makers of the United States.

United States have wrestled with institutional hegemony. The problems of hegemony seem to consist of pigmentation indifference, cultural barriers and hostility among differences whether it is socioeconomic values or anti-social behavior due to traditions, personal or professional background history. Statesmen are paid regardless if policies fail or succeed, and the mass population are victimized by the brutality, abuse, dysfunction and defectiveness of the infrastructure, system and leadership who are not regulated, and corporations who are also not regulated by an equilibrium or equalizer scales.

12th Day Journal Entry: Pity Parties Pitfalls

The day of celebration often comes with the days that are married to pity parties and pitfalls because without rainbows and sunshine(s) come

Moving Wealth

with trials and tribulations even tests in a troubled world. The environmental racism that people are not getting the dignity and respect or values of the wealthy, rich, and popular. We can often times argue that the poor, criminal and insane even hospitalize have been marginalized. We have included other groups that may be described as discriminated against by other factors that are not included on this list as a hardship and challenge, we have set up obstacles in this world to create a dangerous labyrinth. The Merlin and King Arthur symbolism often hold the key to my leadership to leadership model that I created in my Masters Degree program to develop humanity and faith base communities to understand the power of transference, transformation and transcendence that leads to an ascension and ascending life. We have learned that an elevated life means that we can explore and discover and develop each individual as we build brick by brick the roles of universal standards and universal responsibilities that will lead to a restorative accountability system that meet the needs and motivation of all disciplines, belief systems and ideologies. Co-exist is a very important and powerful power support system that can be construed as an innovation to bring safe space to all, and give people the room to grow,

And Moving Into Wealth

Moving Wealth

develop and mature as old growth requires time, and space to occur.

  These celebrations must happen for self-discovery, self-help and self-sustainability. To slow down aging, and to create a world of innovation, creativity and development that invention and reinvention happens; we have to understand the role of celebration. Pity parties happen based on the need and motivation to have desire. The unfulfilled desires create pity. The yearning and lamentation to fulfill desires can be construed based on values, cognitive programming and often suggestive coercing through advertisements, commercialization, consumerism and other mechanism from buying and selling through business. WE often times do not understand the need and motivation to acquire certain products and performances, even services unless we are highly competent in research and investigation. Therefore these skills conclude a high sophistication of knowledge in regarding to quality analysis and quality standards based on certain models and mathematical calculations. These pity parties are lurking in our lives based on the need and motivation to DESIRE goods and services. The ancient times often call these basic needs and basic wants as a process of instinctive relationship we

And Moving Into Wealth

Moving Wealth

have with our environment, communities and with our creator that lives within us as an access channel to celestial and telekinesis models for connection and medium with our cosmic self.

Wealth means having the access and resources to quicken our energy and keep our light shining in the galaxies as the sun to the earth and the moon to the stars. Our cosmic self explores the possibilities to connect on an atomic level to all resources from all planets, solar systems, stars, and energies within the planet earth, biodiversity and biospheres that are located on many dimensions as to fictional imagination adrenaline rush and real-time. This brings me to our modernization globalization economy systems that also build our trust and access to power through the virtual operations as to robotics, technologies and artificial intelligence(s). Let us not forget the power of virtual operations with teleconferencing and mass communication systems that include catalogs, taxonomy and classifications that group data from fictional to real time and beyond. Moving wealth means that we have access to these knowledge bases and also the manifestations of these databases as well under the umbrella of our prescription to digest knowledge and application system of a collective. This collective consciousness was often

And Moving Into Wealth

Moving Wealth

discussed by Dr. Carl Jung. The application system of psychology science may have been excluded from the application system of modern medicine and surgery which we have described this as advanced medicine. Now we have the fortunate world of Neurology science and Sports and Medicine science that have advanced our medical world into the opportunity to use therapy as a health agent and health agencies.

This brings me to my point that pity parties and pitfalls often come with our mortality in our cosmic parallel self. We are wonderful and fearfully engineered and designed by our First Ancestor which often times are called the Alpha and Omega Designer. WE are fortunate to know that no creation or species will out live the Engineer of our Soul. The plans of prosperity is that we have the opportunity to taste this concept of salvation, resurrection, redemption and repentance model through the engineer's standpoint that we can come to an infinite and immortal citizenship that protects us from decay, defects and dysfunction of our brand, model which is who we are as a designed creation. This moving wealth iconic figure can be a loyalty system which is the incentive system of us. We have an incentive system that give us an insurance policy that keep us from falling into the

And Moving Into Wealth

Moving Wealth

trap of the abyss and permanent disconnection of atomic energy which in this wealth we call it the cosmic self. We are the economy system from within our network system and the manifestation is the external wealth network system. These two systems create one marriage, and the cosmic self which is the internal system and the vehicle which is the first estate of our body. Now do want to understand these things on a science or a religious basis as the heaven is to the earth. WE have the astronomical system and the mathematical system. The quantum physics system and the physics system of who we are as a totality and holistic brand. So we have this wellness system that supports the creative ideology of "WHOLENESS and GREATNESS."

      The Pity Parties and Pitfalls celebrates the unification and reconciliation that we no longer mourn, grieve, or complain for that have passed. We no longer fall under the old ways and old system of murmur and groaning. WE have the mediation and access to reconciliation that never happened in the past. This is the new system that engulfs the old system. Moving Wealth is that we can have a new life continuing as a regenerative power source connected to the process of repentance often times comes through the

And Moving Into Wealth

Moving Wealth

manifestation of fasting, meditation and prayers which is the pity parties from the pitfalls of our mortality. The limitation becomes the access to unlimited possibilities after reconciliation and redemption that often times comes from the mediation system and restorative reconciliation system of our cosmic self. The manifestation of our first estate can be construed as having the real time application of our body that concludes that soul of who we are in the essence of the regenerative battery of our cosmic system in our cosmic self. This is the reality that allows imagination and fiction to be our compelling support system that never leaves us or never forsakes us. We now have the economy system that produces concrete evidence that creates reconciliation and resurrection under these laws of attraction system. Now we can call this our new justice system from a cosmic level and a terrestrial model. No longer our terrestrial bodies will be connected to a power source that is considered as a corruptible generator. WE are now connected to a power source that is considered as an incorruptible generator for our energy to be quickened when we are low in morale and low in activity. We are now an active ingredient.

And Moving Into Wealth

Moving Wealth

13th Day Journal Entry: Steadfastness and Will Power

What does it mean to be steadfast and giving will power to your mindfulness and relationship building with your creator? The wealth and moving of wealth means to be able to focus and zoom in on the power transferred from one dimension to the next dimension. The faith that is unseen but evidence that the things shown to your heart, mind and life through signs and wonders gives you the empowerment and the wealth to inherit greater treasures in this life and your daily operating self. We have come so far in life to ignore the very truths and evidences of subtle realities of what we are out of fear that we are going insane. We are convinced that chasing the capitalism in our life is more important than to understand the values of what our cosmic self has the capabilities in doing as though living and ascending from our own destruction, decay and aging. We spend our lives attaining wealth that rot and stays in this world and in this worldly system instead of targeting the power from within us to withstand the entanglements of the destruction traps in this life for our development of our greater self.

I get it that life in this life you want to prove others your worthiness, net worth and capitalism to

And Moving Into Wealth

Moving Wealth

show liberation, power, authority and victor. I have heard of the rumors and seen the mistreatment of all those who have virtues. Those who have spent their lives using their precious time to connect and become one with their creator. I have seen the life they have walked away to live a life of solitude and isolation even alienation from the world as though they died to this world. The daily impact of knowing that you may not get to experience human experiences as social behavior and loving yourself, family and the things in this world. The thought of losing everything to invest in things you do not know if it is a trap or a lie. Steadfastness is not some element that is vain or reach for vanity. It is not something as emptiness or void. It has nothing to do with steadfastness into the darkness of nothingness. It is grasping at the straws given to you to see what the possibilities of what possibly will happen when time matures, when one matures. For instance the concept of streets paved in gold. People say it is a fundamentalist idea that people have been brainwashed by religion to believe in hog wash that streets could be made of gold. And why would it matter when we have earth quakes, tsunamis and other natural disasters to earth that would damage the earth hemisphere as to the beauty created with resources to give our world a beautification against the slushiness of decay and

And Moving Into Wealth

Moving Wealth

destructive behavior that corruption have plagued our worlds to this point.

It is evidence that steadfastness is given by the relationship by the Creator for your mind to be fixated on the things given to one as an inheritance. An active promise to revive you when times are hard, when changes are happening and when enduring great suffering and pain to make it through the trials and tribulations in this life. It is the evidence that your mind holds and steadfast of not giving up in hoping, believing and instead of falsehood but real and evidence given to you by the creator through proof and affirmation in your external as well as your internal world and life. It is the truth that is hidden from others, but shines on your forehead when you are sick, unconscious and subconscious reminding that it would never leave you or forsake you. It is a greater joy that can not be formed from the belly of pleasures in this life. It is given to one by the Creator and the forces of what births your own life into existence. It is something that is not given to others but you. The steadfastness that your will power use to keep you alive to see it to the end as if it is yours to attain and yours to cherish and become one with in this life time through believing and loving its existence in your mind and in your heart. It is not what

And Moving Into Wealth

Moving Wealth

capitalism teach in schools, and it is not what religion teaches in books, yet it may trigger you from those elements of science, humanities and religion to show you that you can see things from within and also see things in all things under the sun as though you do not need a teacher, but teachers and mentors are confirmations and affirmations to your God insurance and God stocks.

   Steadfastness and Will Power are your God stocks and your God insurance policy that you are a stakeholder and under the conditions set before you that you have available the power and riches to set things apart by your decision making in whatever situation or circumstance presented to you. And these confirmations, affirmations and revelations are the resources, riches that are used to provide for your daily needs according to what has been written for your script in your life. Sometimes we can be so positive and that positive gives you the strength to develop and build one's faith. But, what I am talking about is revelations and words from the living Creator of your soul that speaks to your mind and heart so that your life is branded like a horse with a mark that the horse is owned by an owner. We have been pierced by the tattooing of the living God with his words on the written slates of our lives to understand that the riches of what he speaks

And Moving Into Wealth

Moving Wealth

to us are evidence and power to give us a rich and inherited life. Steadfastness and will power becomes that distributions center to the eternal wealth, daily wealth of humanity and celestial worlds at our finger tips. But, many won't use it because of distraction and lack of discipline to keep the target at a point of focus and centering.

14th Day Journal Entry: Raw Talent and Refinement

What happens when you are not given the chance to demonstrate your talent. Your cosmic power? What happens when you are not able to get your talent matured based on the lack of support in your environment and you are unable to sharpen your skills? Today's society I have learned that many communities do not allow people to find safe spaces to train, educate and receive role models, mentors and coaches in their talent or craft. Today it is often sad that our government behavior and corporate behavior have their favorites. We are thrust in a society that ignores those who are not able to rise to the occasion.

I had to prove that SALVATION, RESURRECTION AND REDEMPTION was real and not a figment of our imagination. I had to

And Moving Into Wealth

Moving Wealth

understand the purpose of talent and refinement. We live in this society running to and fro seeking for those to devour. This is the worldviews of tyranny. It is obvious that we have to ask ourselves questions in this life when our environments are hostile and lack of confidence in our system appears to be a fairy tale wonder story for the vulnerability. I spent most of my look seeking for evidence. Concrete evidence that I could use as to tangible things as the trees, birds, ocean, volcano and such. I had a wonderful idea and I started on this journey to use the natural world to be my witnesses and mentors in teaching and lecturing me about salvation, resurrection and redemption. This will be the reason we are given cosmic powers as we call them talent and craft. Why it is important to refine ourselves using self autonomy and self actualization even self transformation. The MOVING WEALTH means in this dimension, how do we move the COSMIC ME, MYSELF and I co-creator of this universal world? I began this journey asking these questions, researching for some evidence and concrete tangible realism that no skeptic could dispute. They could if they just was not interested in MOVING WEALTH as to moving GOD, YAH and now Prince of GOD, YAH Principals and Principles. The Prince of Peace meant for this dimension the Prince of Salvation,

And Moving Into Wealth

Moving Wealth

Resurrection and Redemption. Refining your craft, talent and cosmic power or atomic energy meant to understand how to move wealth; your inheritance in your remarkably created body, soul, spirit as one force: the Billion member living organism system.

The Human Anatomy Universe: You are wonderfully and fearfully Created and Engineered. The Cosmic (Physic, Metaphysics and Quantum Physic) You ---Note: The earth's wealth is less than 800 Trillion dollars, and that is a 21st century short list estimate because we have only valued natural resources as valuable as to: rocks, crystals, minerals and natural elements as to objects. We have excluded human value, and all the species that are living whether registered or not registered. For one minute, think about all the parts of your human anatomy and value it as you would diamond, gold, stainless steel, marble, and other natural elements crystals.

"It is estimated that 500 to 1000 species of bacteria live in the human gut and a roughly similar number on the skin. Bacterial cells are much smaller than human cells, and there are at least ten times as many bacteria as human cells in the body (approximately 10^{14} versus 10^{13}).

The mass of microorganisms is estimated to account for 1-3%

And Moving Into Wealth

Moving Wealth

total body mass.

Though members of the flora are found on all surfaces exposed to the environment (on the skin and eyes, in the mouth, nose, small intestine), the vast majority of bacteria live in the large intestine."

The table below gives the amount of each chemical element found in the human body, from most to least abundant. For each element, there is the amount in mass units in an averge (70-kilogram) person, the volume of the element, and the length of the side of a cube that would contain that amount of the pure element. Volumes of solid and liquid elements are based on density at or near room temperature (where available). For the gaseous elements (oxygen, hydrogen, nitrogen, chlorine, and fluorine), I chose to use the density of each in the liquid state at the respective boiling point.

Raw data from which this table was made are from Emsley, John, The Elements, 3rd ed., Clarendon Press, Oxford, 1998. This is a great trove of information, which I highly recommend for anyone wishing to learn more about the elements.

Element Mass of element
in a 70-kg person Volume of
purified element Element would
comprise a cube
this long
on a side:
oxygen 43 kg 37 L 33.5 cm
carbon 16 kg 7.08 L 19.2 cm

And Moving Into Wealth

Moving Wealth

        hydrogen 7 kg 98.6 L 46.2 cm
        nitrogen 1.8 kg 2.05 L 12.7 cm
        calcium 1.0 kg 645 mL 8.64 cm
        phosphorus 780 g 429 mL 7.54 cm
        potassium 140 g 162 mL 5.46 cm
        sulfur 140 g 67.6 mL 4.07 cm
        sodium 100 g 103 mL 4.69 cm
        chlorine 95 g 63 mL 3.98 cm
        magnesium 19 g 10.9 mL 2.22 cm
        iron 4.2 g 0.53 mL 8.1 mm
        fluorine 2.6 g 1.72 mL 1.20 cm
        zinc 2.3 g 0.32 mL 6.9 mm
        silicon 1.0 g 0.43 mL 7.5 mm
        rubidium 0.68 g 0.44 mL 7.6 mm
        strontium 0.32 g 0.13 mL 5.0 mm
        bromine 0.26 g 64.2 μL 4.0 mm
        lead 0.12 g 10.6 μL 2.2 mm
        copper 72 mg 8.04 μL 2.0 mm
        aluminum 60 mg 22 μL 2.8 mm
        cadmium 50 mg 5.78 μL 1.8 mm
        cerium 40 mg 4.85 μL 1.7 mm
        barium 22 mg 6.12 μL 1.8 mm
        iodine 20 mg 4.06 μL 1.6 mm
        tin 20 mg 3.48 μL 1.5 mm
        titanium 20 mg 4.41 μL 1.6 mm
        boron 18 mg 7.69 μL 2.0 mm
        nickel 15 mg 1.69 μL 1.2 mm
        selenium 15 mg 3.13 μL 1.5 mm
        chromium 14 mg 1.95 μL 1.3 mm
        manganese 12 mg 1.61 μL 1.2 mm
        arsenic 7 mg 1.21 μL 1.1 mm
        lithium 7 mg 13.1 μL 2.4 mm

And Moving Into Wealth

Moving Wealth

cesium 6 mg 3.2 µL 1.5 mm
mercury 6 mg 0.44 µL 0.8 mm
germanium 5 mg 0.94 µL 1.0 mm
molybdenum 5 mg 0.49 µL 0.8 mm
cobalt 3 mg 0.34 µL 0.7 mm
antimony 2 mg 0.30 µL 0.7 mm
silver 2 mg 0.19 µL 0.6 mm
niobium 1.5 mg 0.18 µL 0.6 mm
zirconium 1 mg 0.15 µL 0.54 mm
lanthanium 0.8 mg 0.13 µL 0.51 mm
gallium 0.7 mg 0.12 µL 0.49 mm
tellurium 0.7 mg 0.11 µL 0.48 mm
yttrium 0.6 mg 0.13 µL 0.51 mm
bismuth 0.5 mg 51 nL 0.37 mm
thallium 0.5 mg 42 nL 0.35 mm
indium 0.4 mg 55 nL 0.38 mm
gold 0.2 mg 10 nL 0.22 mm
scandium 0.2 mg 67 nL 0.41 mm
tantalum 0.2 mg 12 nL 0.23 mm
vanadium 0.11 mg 18 nL 0.26 mm
thorium 0.1 mg 8.5 nL 0.20 mm
uranium 0.1 mg 5.3 nL 0.17 mm
samarium 50 µg 6.7 nL 0.19 mm
beryllium 36 µg 20 nL 0.27 mm
tungsten 20 µg 1.0 nL 0.10 mm

Notes

Oxygen is the most abundant element in the earth's crust and in the body. The body's 43 kilograms of oxygen is found mostly as a component of water, which makes up 70% of total body weight. Oxygen is also an integral component of all

And Moving Into Wealth

Moving Wealth

proteins, nucleic acids (DNA and RNA), carbohydrates, and fats.

Rubidium is the most abundant element in the body (0.68 g) that has no known biological role (silicon, which is slightly more abundant, may or may not have a metabolic function).

Vanadium is the body's least abundant element (0.11 mg) that has a known biologic role, followed by cobalt (3 mg), the latter being a constituent of vitamin B12.

The last of the body's elements to be discovered was fluorine, by Moissan in 1886. The human body is a cocktail of at least 58 elements

The average body contains these 4 main elements in these amounts

oxygen 43 kg
carbon 16 kg
hydrogen 7 kg
nitrogen 1.8 kg

Whilst oxygen is the most abundant element at 43 kg it is mostly found as a component of water together with hydrogen which make up 70% of the total body weight. It is also an important element in the composition of RNA, DNA, all proteins, carbohydrates and fats.

However Rubidium is the most abundant element at 0.68 g that has no known biological function within the body.

And Moving Into Wealth

Moving Wealth

There are between 50 and 75 trillion cells in the human body.

Cell types can be classified by their tissue of origin. However, it is possible for some cells to have their behavior induced by surrounding tissue.

Gastrulation is a phase early in the embryonic development of most animals, during which the single-layered blastula is reorganized into a trilaminar ("three-layered") structure known as the gastrula. These three germ layers are known as the ectoderm, mesoderm, and endoderm.

Gastrulation takes place after cleavage and the formation of the blastula and primitive streak. Gastrulation is followed by organogenesis, when individual organs develop within the newly formed germ layers. Each layer gives rise to specific tissues and organs in the developing embryo. The ectoderm gives rise to epidermis, and to the neural crest and other tissues that will later form the nervous system. The mesoderm is found between the ectoderm and the endoderm and gives rise to somites, which form muscle; the cartilage of the ribs and vertebrae; the dermis, the notochord, blood and blood vessels, bone, and connective tissue. The endoderm gives rise to the epithelium of the digestive system and respiratory system, and organs associated with the digestive system, such as the liver and pancreas.

Yahoo Answers/Wikipedia Rough Estimate.

And Moving Into Wealth

Moving Wealth

If we are the little I am as to co-creator, imagine who are first and last ancestor value is in human life or creator's life value of net worth in this system and beyond?

We are empowered and encouraged to use our cosmic talent, skills, power to survive yes indeed. But, also to excel, transcend and overcome. Learning to use our body to work in our favor, refine those experiences and decision making choices means learning how to rise above our ashes. We need to rise up like a Phoenix and bring our fullness and potential under refinement and maturity. Our RAW TALENT AND REFINEMENT becomes our internal fountains and water springs that regenerate our lives. In order to do so, we must understand the complexity of the Merlin and King Arthur living as a symbolic role we have with our Creator and as Co-creators live as one within any environment our bodies travel, co-habitat and live.

What does this means in that our body system is a solar system, galaxy and an atomic system that we call our living system. This anatomy in all its entirety function as a planet even more as a galaxy and universe, in its order and organized behavior, sophisticated management

And Moving Into Wealth

Moving Wealth

system, its operations daily to give us and provides a living system vehicle to channel our expressions, personality and persona energy through as light needs a manifestation, wind need a manifestation; our bodies are our manifestation of our spiritual existence which we call our consciousness. We have not touched the surface to what we can possibly achieved. We are so caught up with the falsehood of premature deaths through violence and havoc, we forfeit our opportunities to achieve the potential usage and mastery of our created forms. Our first estate. So let us begin with the concrete evidence that we have salvation, redemption and resurrection through our evidence of our masterful bodies as a channel and conduit of this life force that we call our persona or spirit; eternal personality.

      The soul is made up of the breath of life and the form we live in which we call our first estate. The breathe is called the spirit which is the personality or son and daughter of God sent to inherit and own a temple which is our body. Our spirit lives in this earthly temple. We have evidence that it is a living system that is 95% chemically base. Interesting enough the other 5% components help us shape and construct the temple into a model. We call that the body or the cup. But our

And Moving Into Wealth

Moving Wealth

spirit, which is the personality and the persona of our consciousness which can be a library or database that we have been given by God our creator, the guidance of our Yah and our own experiences and training, as one collection, we have a collective of infinity of time locked up in our consciousness. We have not learned how to reach our potential of our memory database or knowledge database we call the knowledge of GOD. The totality of all experiences from the beginning of time to the end of time.

      Mostly we have not learn true wealth management or wealth application based on the trouble in the world. WE have been separated from our lessons to discover and master our first estate, the moving of wealth is learning how to move the WHOLE SELF. In that dimension, we cannot learn just of our human or earthly parents and earthly world, but we must also learn of our COSMIC world which is our heavenly parents. We are a mixed breed in the COSMOS. All species look upon us because we have four parents that make up of our total composition. We have our humanity DNA and our COSMIC DNA. They do not teach this in secular schools because they forgot their lessons to learn of their Merlin symbolically speaking (COSMIC mentor YAHWEH). We fear

And Moving Into Wealth

Moving Wealth

what we do not know and do not understand. Therefore we violate and destroy what we do not accept and approve. We lose countenance in doing what is loving and good in this life based on the lack of knowing who we truly are in this cosmos civilization. We are disconnected from our COSMOS civility. We disconnect from our wealth and move away from our wealth based on misunderstanding the values of our role in this life from our COSMOS UNIVERSE.

THE FASHION DESIGN AND THE TARGET PRACTICE: MODULE 3

The Fashion Design and The Target Practice
15th Day Entry: Aesthetics and Editing
16th Day Entry: Finding Your Expression
17th Day Entry: Creating and Playing
18th Day Entry: Duties and Commitments
19th Day Entry: Engagement and Resilience
20th Day Entry: Challenges and Sabotage
21th Day Entry: Trust and Tread Lightly

The Work Ethics and The Life Studies
22th Day Entry: The Custom Fit
23th Day Entry: Tailor Made
24th Day Entry: Mature and Old Growth
25th Day Entry: Diversification and Purity
26th Day Entry: Traditions and Yesterday Lessons

And Moving Into Wealth

Moving Wealth

27th Day Entry: Transformation and Transcending
28th Day Entry: Ascension and Descension

The Journey of Moving Out and The Moving In
29th Day Entry: Saying Goodbye to Old Wealth
30th Day Entry: Good morning: Rise and shine
31th Day Entry: Honeymoon Stage of Wealth
32th Day Entry: The Romance of Wealth
33th Day Entry: The Working Relationship with Wealth
34th Day Entry: Aging with Wealth
35th Day Entry: Renewing of the Vows with Wealth

Move Into Greatness: Crossing Over
And The Contract to Keep You There
36th Day Entry: Creative and Unconditional Wealth
37th Day Entry: Ironing the Clothes of Wealth
38th Day Entry: Crossing the Red Sea
39th Day Entry: Dress Code and the Code of Wealth
40th Day Entry: Never Leave me or Forsake me Wealth
41th Day Entry: The Knowledge of Yah
42th Day Entry: The Understanding of Yah

Module 3 The Fashion Designer and Target Practice

Moving wealth is like a fashion designer in life. We talk so much about financial management, economics on scarcity and wealth. We forget to talk about our wealth within our own lives. The ability to focus on the things you love to do. We

And Moving Into Wealth

Moving Wealth

forget about visualization, and how do we dream the best dreams in life. I have learned over the years we need more libraries and we need more community universities that teach people how to dream big dreams. We forget how to be dreamers. We are so focus in helping others achieve their goals and their way of paying bills seem to fall in the path of gatekeepers who make the rules. These gatekeepers are dream thieves. They focus on self gain profits, assets and returns; financial increases. And they do not mind walking by people who are unfortunate. They do not mind watching people suffer. They are sociopaths with power, capital and assets. They have the power and dominance to create policies that protect them from the social responsibility to manage disparities better by allowing a welfare system that allows people the right and access even enforcement to have healthy communities like they have done for the Parks and Recreation in the Department of Land Bureau. They govern National parks, but the government won't govern landowners who do not meet the codes of ethics for beautification. We do not have the standards to keep all properties, all lands and territories in a healthy state. The people are forced to pay to live on these properties, but they have to work under the living wage. They have to work

And Moving Into Wealth

Moving Wealth

under the competitive wage, and it is okay for them to have no one to turn to for assistance.

We are talking about the lack of enforcement to socially and responsibly manage the health, wellness and fitness of all communities. We force populations to pay for their living as though they do not have a human right to these things in life as to shelter, clothing, food, medical treatment, therapy, transportation, technology, digital technology, recreation and tourism, and other opportunities to give some level of wellness, fitness and healthiness as to alternative healing, fitness clubs, personal training, life coaching sessions, herbal medicinal tools, and the list goes on. These populations are forced to have no representation by the law. The legal system have traded justice for a contaminated system as to the buyers remorse system. We have seen court appointed not care about their reputation to the underprivilege as for their ratings rates for their behavior and performance for their skills and access to justice as though we have added another level of gate keeping. We are expected to support and become patriots for the idealism and ideology that our courage to sacrifice our lives so the rich can keep their capitalism and the poor and working class can be dependent on their mercy. I assure you that

And Moving Into Wealth

Moving Wealth

moving wealth does not mean boycotting and rioting even lobbying the rich, powerful and the educated. It proves to us that we have lack of strategy in the 21st century to use tools that were expired for a season in time. The fact that we need more creativity to keep the balancing scales and checks and balances on our neighborhood watch dogs to the government, corporation and world super powers for war and martial law even corrections as to the prison complex. We are bound to ask why are we moving wealth? Target practice and editing your life as a fashion designer edits their clothing for style and trend, teaches us that we are meant to create and be co-creators. We are faced with the naked truth that capital is not accessible, power is not accessible, and sometimes our vote is not accessible, so what do we do now? The power of within. The power of visualization. The power of exploring the possibilities of creating strategies that make a difference, get people ready for change and interrupt or disturbed the interaction of humanity and the environment by being a paradigm shifter through creativity and artistry or craft. We have to move wealth by moving our mind first into wealth. What does wealth looks like in your mind. Is it poverty in some places. Or resolution to poverty by giving the government a powerful welfare system that allows people free

And Moving Into Wealth

Moving Wealth

access to beautiful communities, furnished homes, and clean water, air and food, clothing and shelter that provides access to the work they do or volunteer work they do undervalued.

It is the ideology that we are target practicing finding the right strategies to match the right concern and the right social issue that can allow us as the populations progress to have access to health, wellness, fitness and good work ethics even civility and mature moral code to function as a green zone world. This life is challenging but the most challenging is the attitudes of those who think that a welfare system is not a right but a privilege. It is the mindset that poverty is punishment for those who do not give up their lives to work and to comply under the dominance and power of their authorities. It is the absence of healing and the absence of freedom to develop, mature and become old growth beings. We are babies under the sun. We do not live billions of years. We may live billions of seconds, but we do not live billions of years. We do not have access to old growth. We do not have access to infinite processing systems. We do not access to the increase of immortality rates. We do not even have access to the right to slow down our aging process. We live in a generation that is completely complacent and approves of the

And Moving Into Wealth

Moving Wealth

ideas of poverty and the working class being undervalued. We have this in the prison system, in the medical system, in the educational system and finally in business whether it be in community institutions or global institutions; we have the complacency that it is not a right to create and to be given free access to the basic needs in humanity. How do we fix this? We cannot count on the rich letting go all of their wealth to change the infrastructure and then go back to the work day to get the world up to code. What do I mean up to code, all homes, buildings, businesses are rehabilitated, renovated, and up to proper green codes. The fact that landscape is not up to code in all territories shows me that we have a government that accepts and approves of abuse and neglect. They blame others the fact they do not have money, but their mismanagement of money proves that they take care of their own family, and that is enough.

And Moving Into Wealth

Moving Wealth

Day 15th Entry: Aesthetics and Editing

Moving wealth becomes an issue of aesthetics and editing the brands of humanity. Moving wealth means we learn how to build from within first. We learn how to take the pain off of the table, and become a painless society not just through drugs and all vices to keep us numb and pain free. WE have to explore the possibilities to use virtual reality gaming systems to practice exposure therapy and if that becomes a way to become a painless society, what happens when we are programmed by wrong access to power and the wrong access to domination and the wrong access to control. Populations can be mislead and deceived in bringing themselves as a community in others harm, like their ancestors based on not knowing how to love deeply and empathy comes from a high EQ or high emotional intelligence. Emotional Intelligence is the ability to be telepathic and to be omnipresent, which means to understand and feel each person's unseen lifestyles and unseen environments that trigger and motivate them to behave. Social behavior is not based on historical and family values like we were led to believe, but it is based on the idealism that people have the right to choose their values. They are bombarded daily on how to keep their own aesthetics and editions

And Moving Into Wealth

Moving Wealth

through selection of what they might be interested based on personal background experiences and education, but overall it is still a personal influence and construction of a very crucial role of privilege and security.

    We have two accesses to capitalism. We have it in the imagination, and we have it in reality through family lineages as we have been born into privilege and security. Populations who are not born into privilege and security will have scarcity and the teaching of scarcity to fit the roles needed as the labor and work force that do not give them a healthy life or healthy lifestyle. Then we have those who are border line trauma patients who have privilege and security but their environments had injuries and prejudices. They cannot function based on self-esteem and self worth. They were undervalued, witness the torture and terrorism of their world getting destroyed or being exploited. They are the populations we call on the borderline. WE do not know which way they will go in their life as far as civility and ethics. Their aesthetics and editing process may be a progress or a detriment to society and to their own selves. The goal of moving wealth is changing the mental game. The mental game is the secret to the vision. The man or woman or child with a vision will not

And Moving Into Wealth

Moving Wealth

perish...be unhealthy. We need to build new visions. We need to build new goals. We need to teach, coach and train people how to develop their minds through visualization as the virtual reality gaming systems, or manually through imagination, creativity and my favorite legends passed on from generations that are like medicine that heals the soul.

The Day 16th Entry: Finding Your Expression

Some populations will call this moving wealth hogwash. It will be seen as a utopia branch instead of the olive branch it was meant to be to all populations to mend their ways by changing the way they see the world. It was learning how to enjoy virtual reality gaming system, filming and broadcasting, newspapers, magazines, and books, all have one element in common, it is a mental structuring on how we program our mind. It is the infrastructure of our mental game. We do not mind using drugs to silence the pain. The price we pay to have a painless society that are eager to die based on pain management. We have to see it in another direction as to finding our own expression. We have expressed our lives through fighting the power. Fighting the power have always been the

And Moving Into Wealth

Moving Wealth

mindset of humanity. We have never seen any species fight the power but our own species. Humanity seem to not care that we have no rights to fight the power as the animal kingdom or the plant kingdom. We have the bird kingdom and reptile kingdom and all of them cannot afford to fight the power unless they are equally yoked. Otherwise, the lions eat the deer and if they are caught they kill and prey on them daily. WE have that in our powers, principles in our world that we cannot fight the power unless we are sacrificing our life. WE expect to save one and lose one. WE are expected to be defeated, and bullied.

      We live in a hypocritical world that lends a helping hand while biting the hand for access to power, dominance and control. Expression is not a way of receiving liberty. It is a way to monitor and investigate the ones who are exploited. It is a war technique to monitor populations through behavior. The more freedom populations have the more access to monitor and regulate their behavior through social control and dominance by knowing their behavior, habits, patterns and motivations even their weaknesses. Our expression is nothing more than the inability to hide. We can be exploited to program others to lose their own freedoms by ajoining others in the same expression. We are then

And Moving Into Wealth

Moving Wealth

grouped, categorized and labeled as an object. We are given this objectification process through our groups that we are categorized, classified and taxonomy into a world of monitoring for behavior control to provide free access to labor and control. We have seen this done throughout history. The problem in all of this is that the stewardship is poor quality. They mislead people by selling their basic needs to the highest bidder. They are shipped off in these slums and ghettos to experience this prison complex we call the school to prison complex. We are faced with sex trafficking and human trafficking based on the realism that the highest bid wins our life. This invisible society and citizenship comes at the highest bid. WE are given freedom to be exposed. WE are given access to expression to be ransom into a life and community that we are bound to until we die. It is not an accident that we are coerced into the graphics and obligation of our external self. WE hardly resort to the inner self. Moving wealth is learning how to access to the inner wealth and then apply it in the daily operations of our trauma, injuries, and failures in this life as a poverty stricken community and a working class group. WE have to understand how to have creativity in the mind while we are in trauma, triggered and injured. WE no longer have access to visualization and imagination. The

And Moving Into Wealth

Moving Wealth

powers in the external world figured it out that books are knowledge, and knowledge is powerful, but visualization and imagination even creativity are all greater that make knowledge appear to be the new born to the parents of visualization and imagination. The fact that we do not understand these elements in love, life and business; we are faced the naked truth that we are doomed to repeat the cycle without the thoughts of our imagination and visualization for greater strategies and integration and merging of those visual concepts of what I call the green zone lifestyle, community and world.

Our breaking the chains mean moving wealth in our mind first, build the security and safety system, and see achievements and accomplishments becomes the strategy and the lifestyles of the green zone new world. WE cannot take that to a place of merge and integration without stating that expression is not what we do within our external world, but what we do in our internal secrets of our hearts, minds and guts.

And Moving Into Wealth

Moving Wealth

To Be Continued...Stay tuned for Book 2 Moving Wealth
And Moving into Wealth

And Moving Into Wealth

www.ingramcontent.com/pod-product-compliance
Lightning Source LLC
Chambersburg PA
CBHW071422220526
45469CB00004B/1384